Rhinos

Rhinos

Peter Murray

THE CHILD'S WORLD®, INC.

Published in the United States of America by The Child's World®, Inc.
PO Box 326
Chanhassen, MN 55317-0326
800-599-READ
www.childsworld.com

Product Manager Mary Berendes
Editor Katherine Stevenson
Designer Mary Berendes
Contributor Bob Temple

Photo Credits
ANIMALS ANIMALS © Khalid Ghani: 16
ANIMALS ANIMALS © Michael Dick: 13
© Anthony Bannister, The National Audubon Society Collection/Photo Researchers: 26
© Art Wolfe, The National Audubon Society Collection/Photo Researchers: 23
© Daniel J. Cox/naturalexposures.com: 15, 30
© Dieter & Mary Plage/Bruce Coleman, Inc.: 29
© Joe McDonald/www.hoothollow.com: 20
© 1999 Kevin Schafer: 10
© 1994 Mark J. Thomas/Dembinsky Photo Assoc. Inc.: 6
© Mary Ann McDonald/www.hoothollow.com: cover
© 1997 Mike Barlow/Dembinsky Photo Assoc. Inc.: 2
© 2000 Mike Barlow/Dembinsky Photo Assoc. Inc.: 9
© Nigel Dennis, The National Audubon Society Collection/Photo Researchers: 24
© 2000 Wendy Dennis/Dembinsky Photo Assoc. Inc.: 19

Library of Congress Cataloging-in-Publication Data
Murray, Peter, 1952 Sept. 29-
Rhinos / by Peter Murray.
p. cm.
Includes index.
ISBN 1-56766-881-X (library bound : alk. paper)
1. Rhinoceroses—Juvenile literature. [1. Rhinoceroses.] I. Title.
QL737.U63 M87 2001
599.66'8—dc21
00-010781

On the cover...

Front cover: This black rhino lives on the Masai Mara Game Reserve in Kenya.
Page 2: This adult black rhino is watching the photographer take its picture.

Table of Contents

The hot afternoon sun beats down on the African grassland. Tall grass waves in the warm wind. Birds chatter as they fly from place to place. In the distance, some birds are sitting on a large, gray rock. Suddenly the "rock" begins to move and rumble and snort. It isn't a rock at all—it's a rhinoceros!

What Are Rhinoceroses?

Rhinoceroses are called "rhinos" for short. They belong to a group of animals called **mammals.** Mammals have hair on their bodies and feed their babies milk from their bodies. Dogs, cows, and people are mammals, too. Most mammals have lots of hair on their bodies—but not rhinos. Rhinos have hair only on the ends of their tails and on the tips of their ears.

This black rhino is standing still as it watches the photographer. ⇒

Rhinos have thick, wrinkled skin and big, strong legs. In fact, each of a rhino's legs is bigger around than your body! Rhinos are very strong and have heavy bodies. Some rhinos weigh more than a car.

All rhinos have a large horn at the end of their nose. A rhino's horn is made of **keratin,** the same material that makes up your hair and fingernails. Some rhinos have two horns. The front horn (on the tip of the rhino's nose) is usually the longest. Rhino horns are pointed and dangerous.

⇐ Here you can easily see this black rhino's beautiful horns.

Are There Different Kinds of Rhinos?

There are five different kinds, or **species**, of rhinos. *Black rhinos* and *white rhinos* live in Africa. Despite their names, both types are actually gray. Like all rhinos, they like to wallow in the mud on hot days. The mud protects their skin from sunburn and biting insects. It also stains their skin the same gray color as the mud.

Black rhinos have a pointed upper lip. They have nasty tempers and like to live by themselves. *Javan rhinos* are smaller and have thick folds of gray skin. *Sumatran rhinos* are even smaller and have something other rhinos don't—hair all over their bodies.

Here you can see the hair that covers this Sumatran rhino's body. ⇒

White rhinos are the biggest rhinos in the world. Adults stand over six feet high at the shoulder and are more than 16 feet long! Elephants are the only land animals larger than white rhinos. Unlike black rhinos, white rhinos have a square upper lip. They also have a large hump on the back of the neck. White rhinos live on the African plains in small groups called **herds.**

This huge white rhino lives in Kenya. ⇒

Indian rhinos live in northern India. They have only one horn. Their thick, folded skin is covered with knobby bumps and looks like a suit of armor. Indian rhinos live in elephant grass that grows up to 25 feet tall. As they walk along, the rhinos crush the grass, making tunnels everywhere they go.

Indian rhinos have been so heavily hunted that there are fewer than a thousand left alive. Some countries have started to protect these rhinos. India and Nepal have set up special nature areas called **reserves.** There Indian rhinos can live, eat, and raise their babies safely.

⇐ This Indian rhino is nibbling on some grass in a reserve in India.   17

What Do Rhinos Eat?

All rhinos are plant-eaters. They like to eat in the early morning and evening, when the sun isn't as hot. White rhinos eat mostly grass and spend most of their time grazing. They use the hard edges of their square lips to clip off grass in bite-size clumps.

Black and Indian rhinos use their pointed upper lips to eat more than just grass. By using their lips like fingers, they grab small branches and twigs and pull them into their mouths.

Here you can see this black rhino's pointed top ⇒
lip as it eats some branches in South Africa.

Like many animals, male rhinos have a **territory,** an area of land they protect as their own. Male rhinos don't like other male rhinos coming into their territory. When two males meet at the edges of their territories, they stare at each other with their horns almost touching. Sometimes the rhinos fight, but usually they back away and wipe their horns on the ground. Then they come back and stare at each other again. They might do this for an hour or more! After a while, each rhino returns to his own territory.

⇐ These two male white rhinos are having a staredown in Kenya.

What Are Baby Rhinos Like?

A female rhinoceros gives birth to only one baby, or **calf,** at a time. When it is born, the rhino calf doesn't have any horns. Instead, it has one or two smooth, flat spots on top of its nose. Over time, a horn grows from each flat spot.

While a calf is still small, it is in danger of being eaten by lions or other enemies. But the baby has some great protection—its mother! Mother rhinos defend their calves fiercely. Few animals are willing to face an angry mother rhino!

This baby black rhino was born in a zoo in Africa. ⇒

Baby rhinos grow very slowly. For two or three years, the calf stays with its mother. By watching, it learns how to stay safe and where to find food. When the mother is ready to have another baby, the first calf goes off on its own. It is big enough now to defend itself and survive on its own.

Rhinos don't have good eyesight. As they watch for danger, they swing their huge heads back and forth, looking with one eye and then the other. But rhinos' other senses help them stay safe. Rhinos have a very good sense of smell, and their hearing is even better. Their ears move in different directions as the rhinos listen for danger.

If an enemy gets too close, a rhino grunts, snorts, and grumbles. Often this scares the other animal away. But if the enemy won't give up, the angry rhino often charges at it. Rhinos can move quickly for their size— up to 30 miles per hour!

⇐ This black rhino is charging in South Africa.

Do Rhinos Have Enemies?

Baby rhinos are in danger of being attacked and eaten by other animals, such as lions. Adult rhinos are well able to protect themselves against other animals. People are rhinos' biggest enemy. For hundreds of years they have hunted rhinos, especially for their horns. In some parts of the world, rhino horns are used in medicines.

All five rhino species are now in danger of becoming **extinct,** or completely dying out. Two species, the Sumatran rhino and the Javan rhino, are in the greatest danger. But even counting all five species, there are only about 14,000 wild rhinos left in the world.

This rare Javan rhino lives in Indonesia. ⇒

Thousands of years ago, many different kinds of rhinos roamed the earth. Today, the five species that are left are in great danger. Nature reserves and laws against hunting are a good start to helping these animals rebuild their numbers. Learning more about rhinos and working to protect them will help make sure these fascinating creatures will be with us for a long time to come.

⇐ Park workers in Kenya sawed off this white rhino's horns to protect it from poachers. They hope that without its horns, this animal will be left alone.

Glossary

calf (KAFF)
A baby rhino is called a calf. Rhino mothers stay close to their calves and protect them.

extinct (ex-TINKT)
When a kind of animal becomes extinct, it dies out completely. Two rhino species are almost extinct.

herds (HERDZ)
Herds are groups of animals that live together. White rhinos live in herds.

keratin (KEHR-eh-tin)
Keratin is a substance that makes up hair and fingernails. A rhino's horn is made of keratin.

mammals (MAM-mullz)
Mammals are animals that are warm blooded, have hair or fur, and feed their babies milk from their bodies. Rhinos are mammals, and so are people.

reserves (ree-ZERVZ)
Reserves are protected areas of land set aside for animals to live. Some countries have set up reserves for rhinos.

species (SPEE-sheez)
A species is a separate kind of an animal. There are five different species of rhinos.

territory (TEHR-ih-tor-ee)
A territory is an area of land that an animal claims as its own. Male rhinos have territories that they defend against other males.

Index

Web Sites

http://www.rhinos-irf.org

http://www.sosrhino.org

http://www.rhinotrust.org